Gross Things: About Animals

Sarah Russell

Contents

Animals Are Gross

You might think that animals are cute but some animals are really **gross**. Animals can be **gross** in lots of different ways.

Get ready to read about some of the **gross** things that animals do.

Before we start, you need to know this. Some animals **regurgitate** their food. Other animals vomit or make **slime** to get away from **predators**. There are even animals that eat poo and suck blood.

Regurgitators

Some animals regurgitate their food. Most animals do this as a way of feeding their young. Even though it seems pretty gross, the young animals would not survive if they did not get food in this way.

This bird regurgitates food to feed its hungry chick.

Birds that regurgitate food for their young find food and store it in their **crop**. Then, they fly back to their nest to feed their chicks. The birds bring the food back up into their mouths, and the chicks eat it from there!

Some birds regurgitate to feed their young because they have to fly long distances to find food. If they didn't store food in their crop, they might drop it or another bird might take it!

Hummingbirds feed their young regurgitated nectar and insects from their mouth. After searching for food and storing it in their crop, the hummingbirds fly back to their nest to feed their hungry chicks.

This hummingbird is feeding on nectar.

This hummingbird is feeding its chicks regurgitated food.

Cows regurgitate too, but they don't regurgitate food to feed their young. Cows regurgitate because the food they eat – grass, hay and leaves – is hard to **digest**.

Cows eat grass, hay and leaves.

Cows have one stomach that has four digestive **compartments**. After cows swallow their food, the food moves through the first two compartments. Cows then regurgitate the food before swallowing it again. After that, the food passes through the third and fourth compartments where it is properly digested.

Cows have four digestive compartments.

Vomiters

Do you want to know something really weird? Some animals vomit to protect themselves from predators. **Gross!**

Fulmars are vomiters. They are so gross that their name means "foul gull".

fulmar

When adult fulmars are out looking for fish, fulmar chicks have to protect themselves. They **projectile** vomit orange oil all over any predators that come near them. The oil sticks the predator's feathers together, making it difficult for them to fly away.

This fulmar chick is vomiting orange oil.

Gross Fact 2

The fulmar's orange oil stinks like rotten fish.

Turkey vultures also vomit to protect themselves from predators. Their vomit is made up of meat they have eaten. This half-eaten meat smells so disgusting that it stops most predators from coming near their nests.

Turkey vultures eat dead animals.

These turkey vulture chicks are in their nest.

Turkey vultures also regurgitate their food to feed their young. That means they are vomiters *and* regurgitators – **double gross!**

Slime Makers

Let's take a look at another animal that does something extra gross when predators try to bite it. This animal is the hagfish, and it makes slime to protect itself!

This scientist is holding up a hagfish and its slime.

This hagfish is lying on the ocean floor.

Hagfish live on the ocean floor. They eat the bodies of dead sea animals, such as whales and sharks.

Hagfish keep safe from predators by using slime to protect themselves. They make the slime using special **glands** that are found along their body.

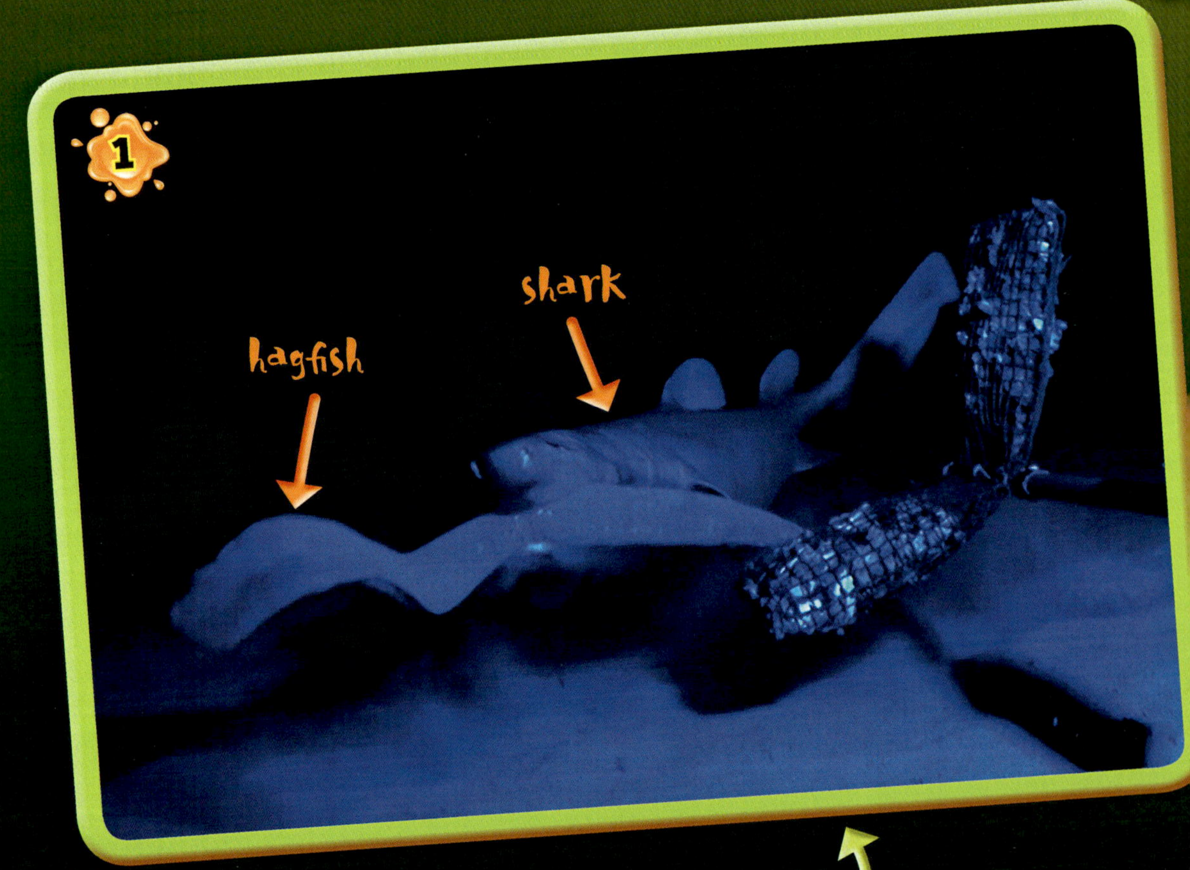

This hagfish is protecting itself from the shark with slime!

The shark is covered in slime.

When a predator tries to bite it, the hagfish covers the predator's mouth and gills in slime. The predator has to let go of the hagfish or it will be **suffocated** by the slime.

Poo Eaters

Now let's take a look at animals that eat poo. Yes, you read that right – some animals eat poo!

Some plants eat poo, too! The pitcher plant is one of them. Pitcher plants eat the poo of small animals called tree shrews.

Tree shrews use the plants as a toilet, and the plants use the poo as food. **Gross!**

Believe it or not, rabbits are poo eaters. Like cows, rabbits eat grass and leaves, which are hard to digest. But unlike cows, rabbits don't regurgitate their food and chew it again.

Rabbits do two kinds of poo:

- a hard poo which has waste in it
- a soft poo which has **nutrients** in it.

They eat their soft poo so they can digest the nutrients further. **Gross!**

Gross Fact 4

Rabbits eat the soft poo straight after they've pooed it!

Dung beetles are insects that eat poo. They don't eat their own poo but they do eat the poo of other animals. These animals eat grass and leaves.

Some dung beetles roll the poo into big round balls. They store the balls of poo and feed on them later.

Dung beetles roll poo into balls.

This is a dung beetle's home. It is made from poo.

Other dung beetles don't bother rolling the poo into balls. They just bury the poo or eat it as soon as they find it. Some dung beetles even live in poo. **Gross!**

Gross Fact 5

Some dung beetles hang around animals' bottoms waiting for them to poo. Then, they roll the poo away and store it so they can eat it later.

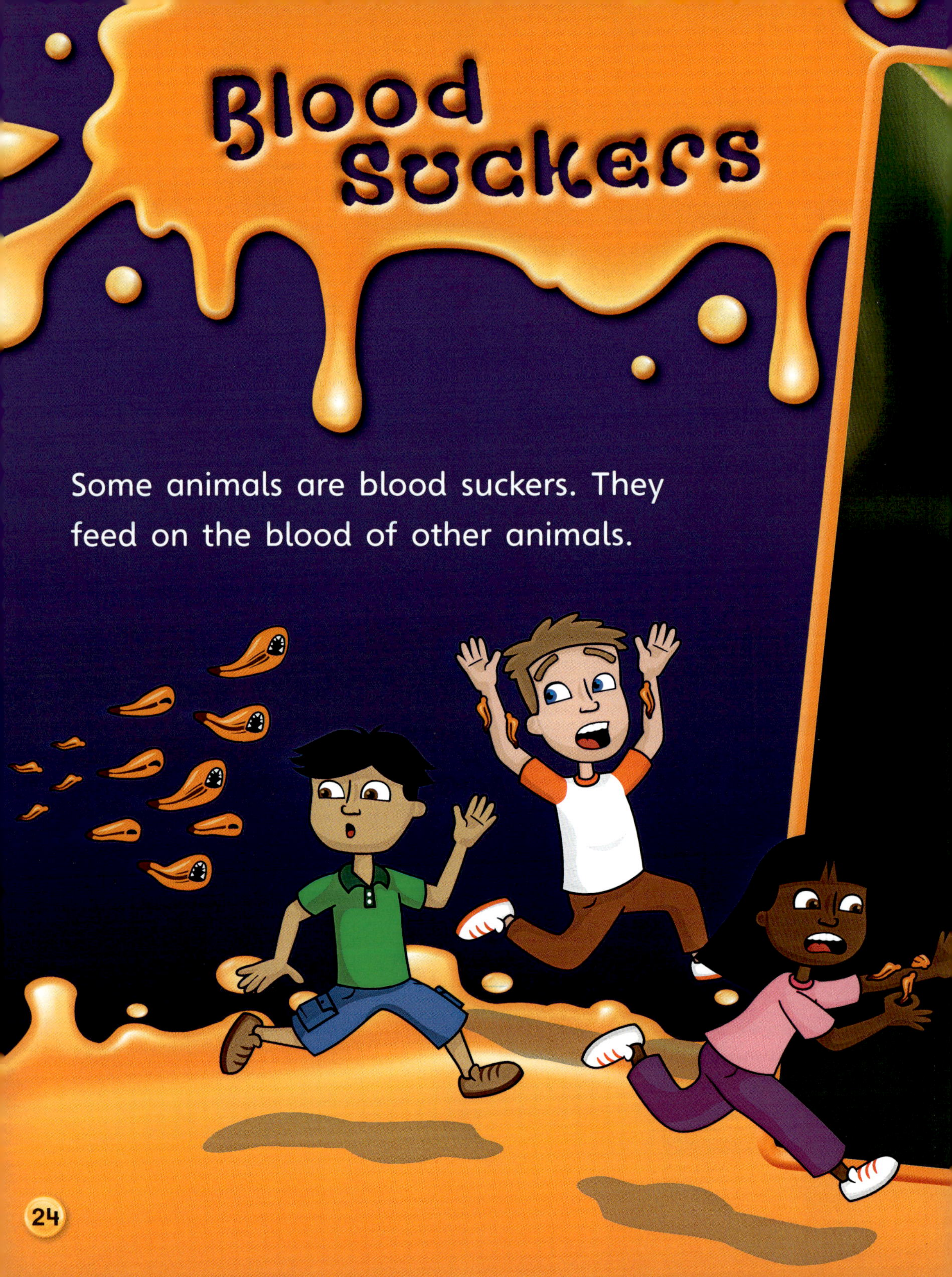

Blood Suckers

Some animals are blood suckers. They feed on the blood of other animals.

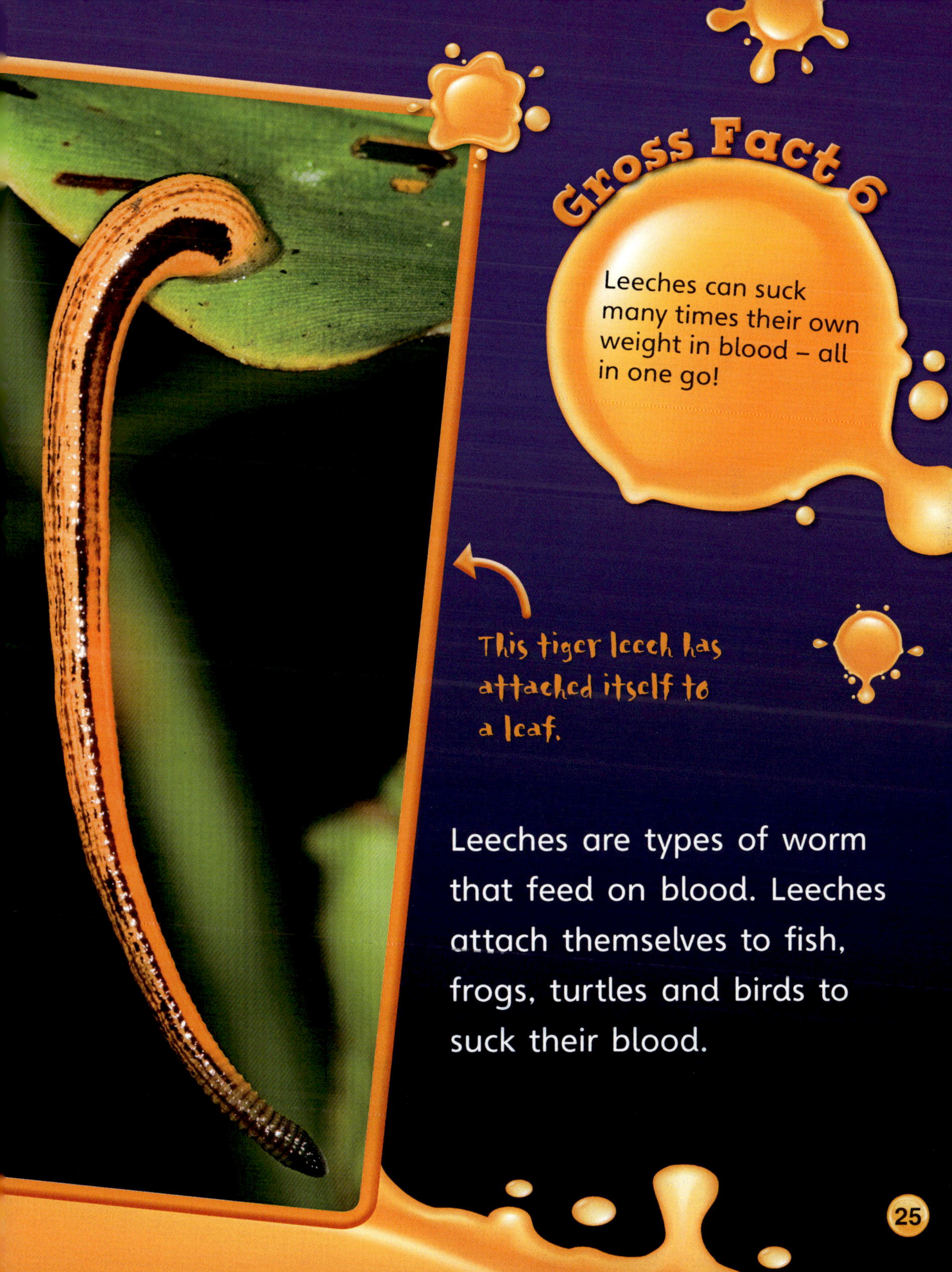

Gross Fact 6

Leeches can suck many times their own weight in blood – all in one go!

This tiger leech has attached itself to a leaf.

Leeches are types of worm that feed on blood. Leeches attach themselves to fish, frogs, turtles and birds to suck their blood.

Some vampire bats feed only on blood. These vampire bats feed on the blood of **mammals** or birds.

vampire bat

Vampire bats find a warm spot on the sleeping animal. Then they bite into the spot and lap up the blood. They can drink up to half their body weight at one time.

Gross Fact 7

Some mosquitoes, flies and butterflies feed on blood, too!

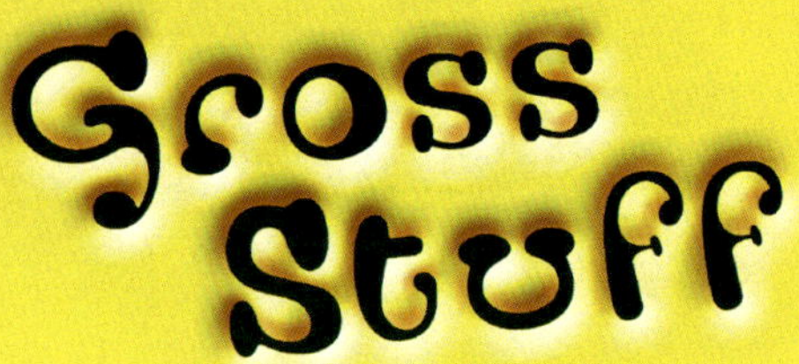

How much **gross stuff** do you remember?
Try this **Gross Quiz**.

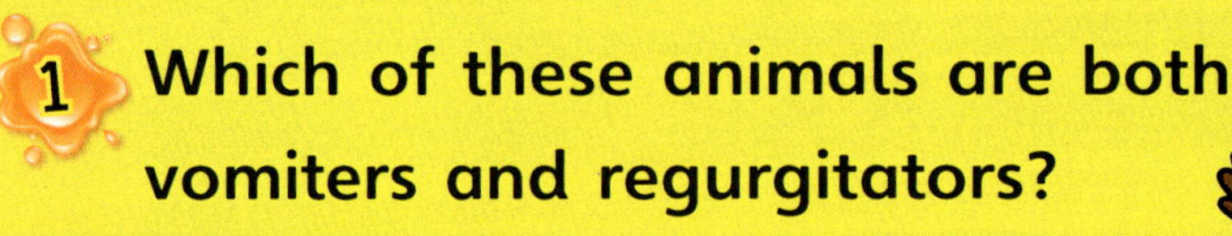

1 **Which of these animals are both vomiters and regurgitators?**

a leeches
b turkey vultures
c vampire bats

2 **Which of these animals make slime?**

a cows
b hummingbirds
c hagfish

3 **Leeches attach themselves to which animals?**

a fish, frogs, turtles and birds

b birds, pigs, dogs and cows

c sheep, cattle, zebras and giraffes

Gross Quiz Answers
1 b **2** c **3** a

All Things Gross!

Well done! You made it to the end of our really disgusting journey. You are now an expert on all things gross about animals! Tell a friend. **Gross them out!**

Glossary

compartments	separate areas or sections
crop	a pouch near the throat of some animals, such as birds, which is used to store food
digest	to break down food in the stomach so it can be used to nourish the body
fibre	a fine, thread-like piece of something
glands	a group of cells that make something the body needs to work
gross	revolting, disgusting
mammals	animals that are fed on milk by their mother
mucus	a slimy, slippery substance
nutrients	things like vitamins and minerals that provide energy
predators	animals that live by feeding on other animals
projectile	something that is thrown forward with force
regurgitate	to bring back to the mouth from the stomach
slime	a thick, sticky, slippery substance
suffocated	lack of air or inability to breathe

Index